MAST. THE ARABIC ALPHABET

A Handwriting Practice Workbook

Perfect Your Calligraphy Skills and Dominate the Modern Standard Arabic Script

by Lang Workbooks

Important Legal Information:

This workbook is a labor of love. Accordingly, if you are a teacher, a student of Arab, or homeschooling your children, *I grant you the non-commercial right to photocopy any part of this workbook for your own, or your students, personal use.*

All further rights are reserved © 2020.

ISBN: 9781653392957

ي

يَاء

Yaa

Y

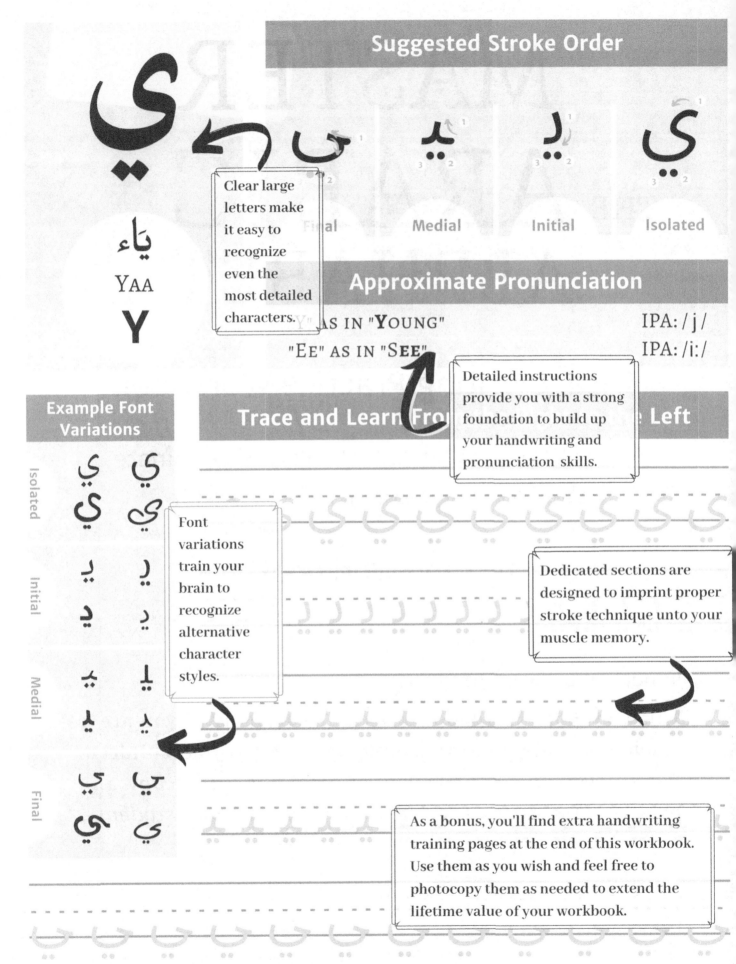

Suggested Stroke Order

Final	Medial	Initial	Isolated
ـي	ـيـ	يـ	ي

Approximate Pronunciation

"Y" as in "**Y**oung" IPA: /j/

"Ee" as in "S**ee**" IPA: /i:/

Example Font Variations

Isolated: ي ي ي ي

Initial: يـ يـ يـ يـ

Medial: ـيـ ـيـ ـيـ ـيـ

Final: ـي ـي ـي ـي

Trace and Learn From Right to Left

Clear large letters make it easy to recognize even the most detailed characters.

Detailed instructions provide you with a strong foundation to build up your handwriting and pronunciation skills.

Font variations train your brain to recognize alternative character styles.

Dedicated sections are designed to imprint proper stroke technique unto your muscle memory.

As a bonus, you'll find extra handwriting training pages at the end of this workbook. Use them as you wish and feel free to photocopy them as needed to extend the lifetime value of your workbook.

Workbook Index

أَلِف
ALIF
Ā

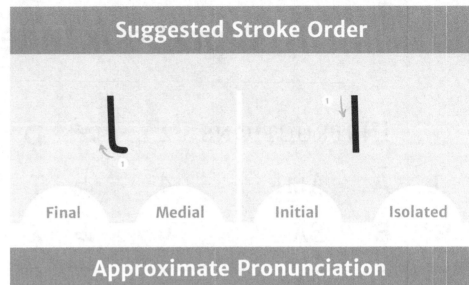

Final   Medial   Initial   Isolated

Approximate Pronunciation

"A" AS IN "ASK"   IPA: /aː/

Example Font Variations

Isolated

ا   ا

ا   ا

Initial

Medial

ل   ل

ل   ل

Final

Trace and Learn From the Right to the Left

بَاء
BAA
B

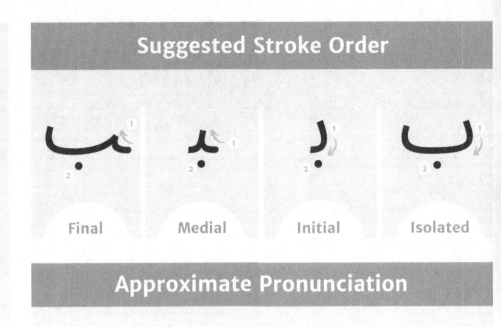

Final | Medial | Initial | Isolated

Approximate Pronunciation

"B" AS IN "**B**ILL"   IPA: /b/

Trace and Learn From the Right to the Left

Isolated

Initial

Medial

Final

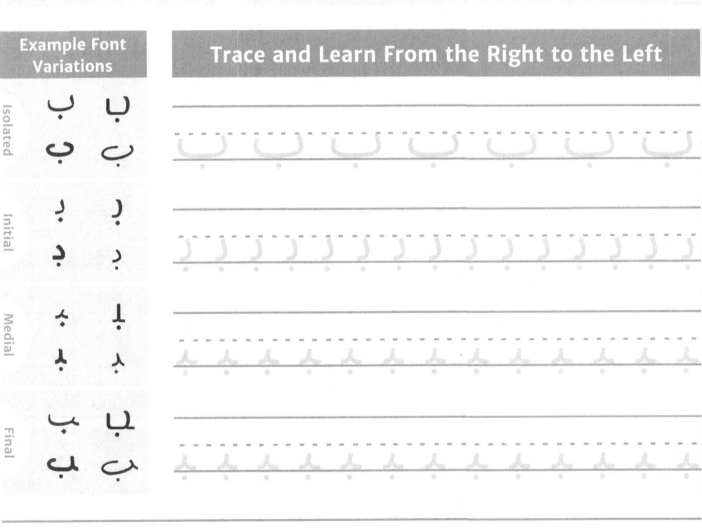

ب ب ب ب ب ب ب ب ب ب ب

ب

ب

ب

ر ر ر ر ر ر ر ر ر ر ر ر ر ر ر ر ر ر ر

ب

ب

ر

ت

Suggested Stroke Order

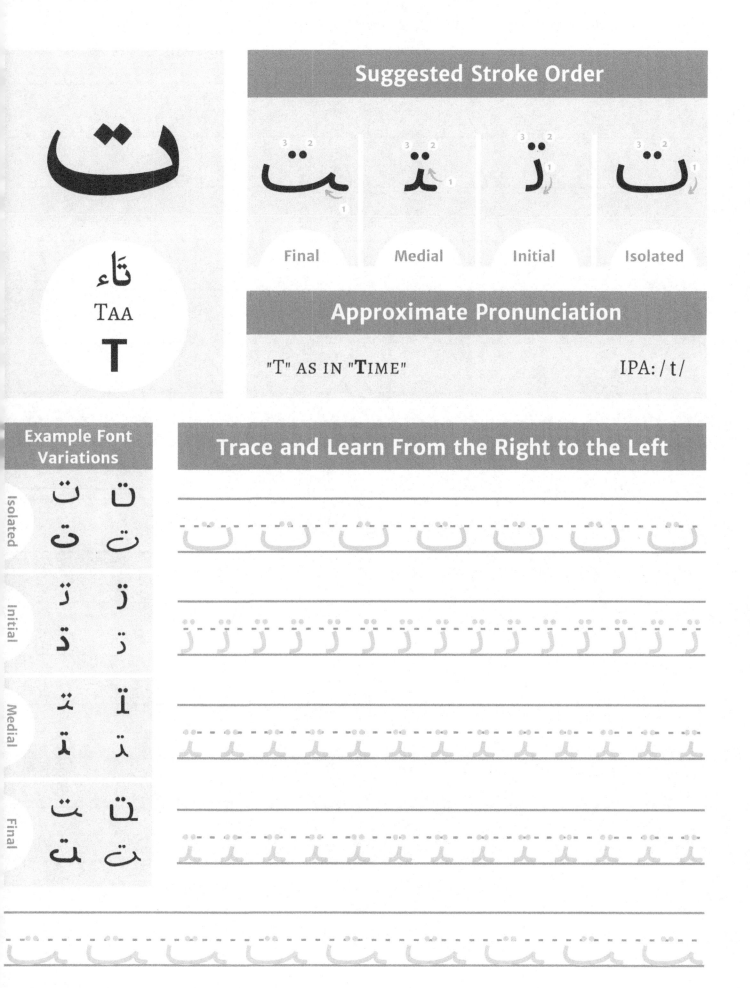

Final Medial Initial Isolated

Approximate Pronunciation

"T" AS IN "TIME"   IPA: / t /

Example Font Variations

Isolated

Initial

Medial

Final

Trace and Learn From the Right to the Left

ت

ت

ث

ت

ڗ

ڗ

ڗ

ڗ

ﺕ ﺕ ﺕ ﺕ ﺕ ﺕ ﺕ ﺕ ﺕ ﺕ ﺕ ﺕ ﺕ ﺕ ﺕ ﺕ ﺕ ﺕ

ﺕ

ﺕ

ﺕ

ﺙ ﺙ ﺙ ﺙ ﺙ ﺙ ﺙ ﺙ ﺙ ﺙ

ﺙ

ﺙ

ﺙ

ﺙ

ثَاء

THAA

Th

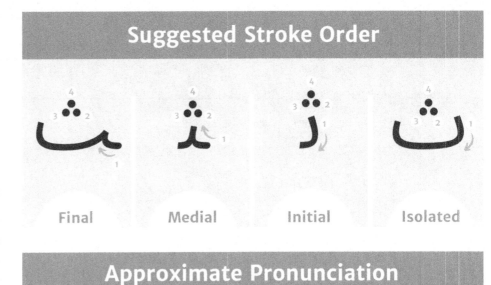

Final   Medial   Initial   Isolated

Approximate Pronunciation

"TH" AS IN "**TH**INK"   IPA: /θ/

Example Font Variations	

Isolated	ث	ﺙ
	ث	ﺙ
Initial	ﺛ	ﺛ
	ﺛ	ﺛ
Medial	ﺜ	ﺌ
	ﺜ	ﺌ
Final	ﺚ	ﺚ
	ﺚ	ﺚ

Trace and Learn From the Right to the Left

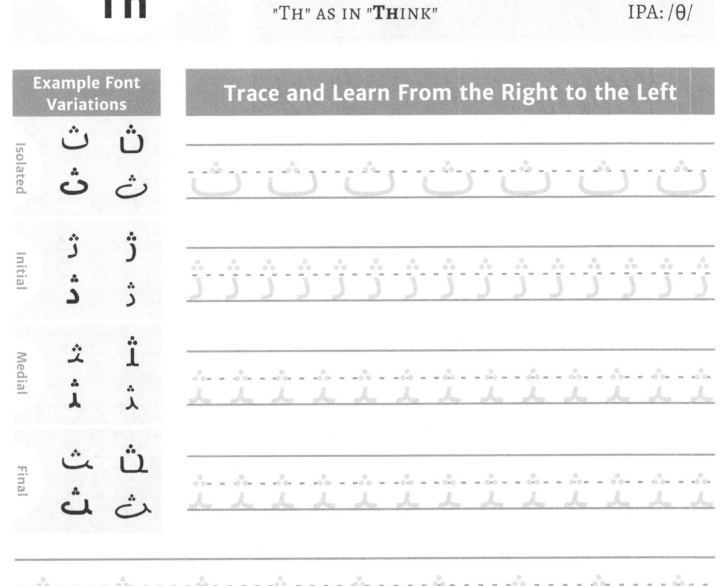

ثْ ثْ ثْ ثْ ثْ ثْ ثْ ثْ ثْ ثْ ثْ

ثْ

ثْ

ثْ

ﺛ ﺛ ﺛ ﺛ ﺛ ﺛ ﺛ ﺛ ﺛ ﺛ ﺛ ﺛ ﺛ ﺛ

ﺛ

ﺛ

ﺛ

جِيم

JEEM

ج

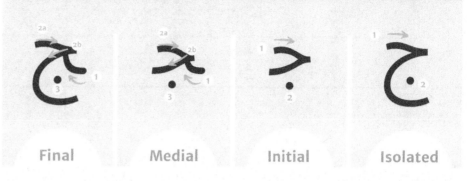

| Final | Medial | Initial | Isolated |

Approximate Pronunciation

"G" AS IN "**G**EM"   IPA: /d͡ʒ/

"G" AS IN "**G**IRL" IN EGYPTIAN ARABIC   IPA: /g/

Example Font Variations

Trace and Learn From the Right to the Left

Isolated

Initial

Medial

Final

ぇ ぇ ぇ ぇ ぇ ぇ ぇ ぇ ぇ ぇ ぇ ぇ ぇ

ぇ

ぇ

ぇ

て て て て て て て て て て て て て

て

て

て

て

حَاءُ

ḤAA

Ḥ

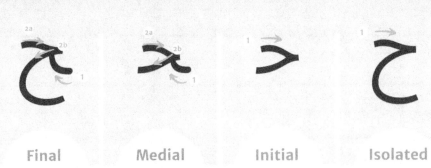

Final   Medial   Initial   Isolated

Approximate Pronunciation

SIMILAR TO THE "H" IN "**H**EART"
BUT WITH A GUTTURAL SOUND

IPA: /ħ/

Example Font Variations

Isolated	
Initial	
Medial	
Final	

Trace and Learn From the Right to the Left

ح ح ح ح ح ح ح ح ح ح ح ح ح ح ح

ح

ح

ح

ز ز ز ز ز ز ز ز ز ز ز ز ز ز ز

ز

ز

ز

ぇ ぇ ぇ ぇ ぇ ぇ ぇ ぇ ぇ ぇ ぇ ぇ ぇ ぇ ぇ

ぇ

ぇ

ぇ

て て て て て て て て て て て て て て て

て

て

て

て

خَاء

KHAA

Kh

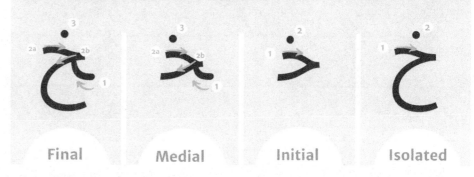

Final   Medial   Initial   Isolated

Approximate Pronunciation

"CH" AS IN THE GERMAN
NAME "BaCH"

IPA: /x/

Example Font Variations

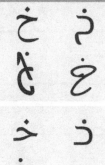

Isolated

Initial

Medial

Final

Trace and Learn From the Right to the Left

ح ح ح ح ح ح ح ح ح ح ح ح ح ح

ح

خ

خ

ذ ذ ذ ذ ذ ذ ذ ذ ذ ذ ذ ذ ذ ذ

ذ

ذ

ذ

خ خ خ خ خ خ خ خ خ خ خ خ خ خ

خ

خ

خ

ح ح ح ح ح ح ح ح ح ح ح ح ح ح

خ

خ

خ

خ

د

دَال
DAAL
D

Final   Medial   Initial   Isolated

Approximate Pronunciation

"D" AS IN "**D**ICE"   IPA: /d/

Example Font Variations

Isolated

Initial

Medial

Final

Trace and Learn From the Right to the Left

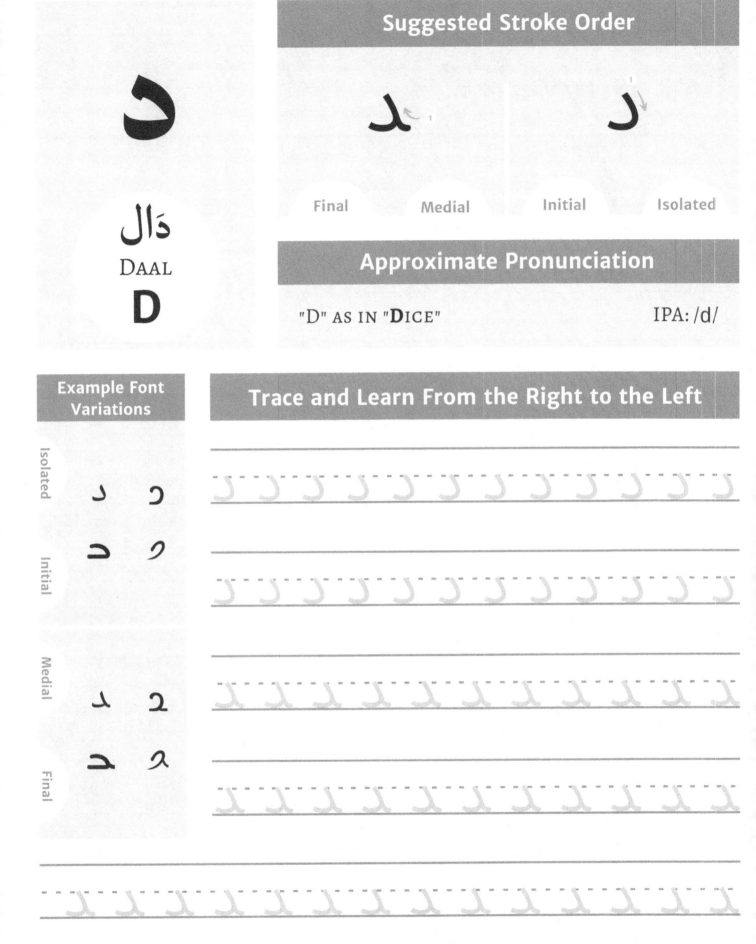

ى ى ى ى ى ى ى ى ى ى ى ى ى ى ى ى ى ى

ى

ى

ى

لا لا لا لا لا لا لا لا لا لا لا لا لا لا لا لا

لا

لا

لا

لا

ذ

ذَال

DHAAL

Dh

Final　　　Medial　　　Initial　　　Isolated

Approximate Pronunciation

"TH" AS IN "THIS"　　　　　　　　IPA: /ð/

Example Font Variations

Isolated

Initial

Medial

Final

Trace and Learn From the Right to the Left

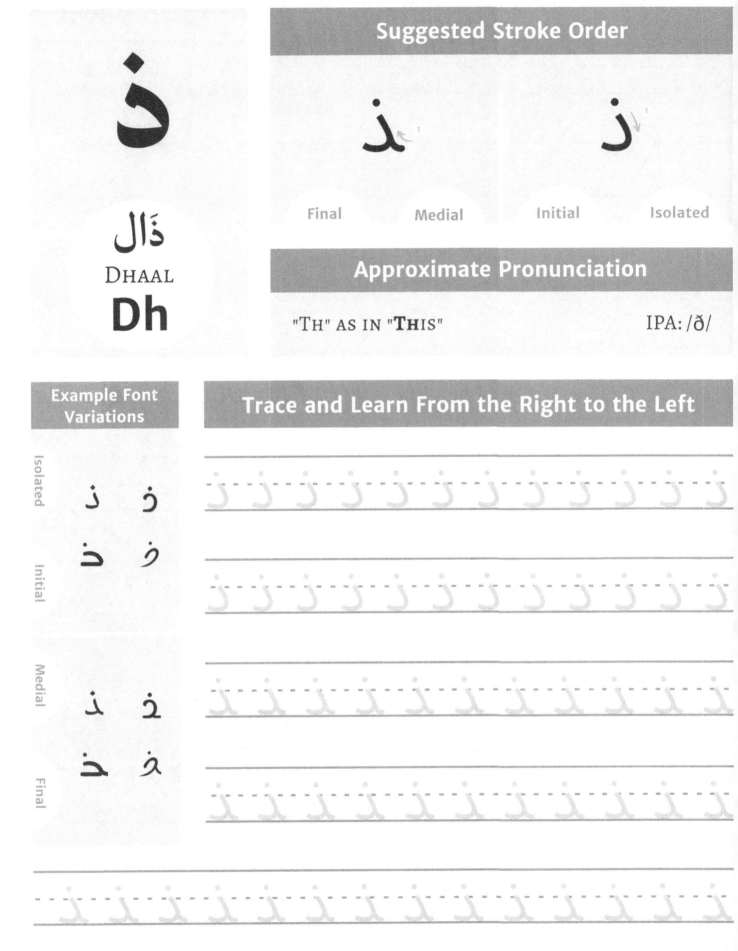

ذ ذ ذ ذ ذ ذ ذ ذ ذ ذ ذ ذ ذ ذ ذ ذ ذ

ذ

ذ

ذ

ذذ ذذ ذذ ذذ ذذ ذذ ذذ ذذ ذذ ذذ ذذ ذذ ذذ ذذ ذذ

ذذ

ذذ

ذذ

ر

دَاء
RAA

R

Suggested Stroke Order

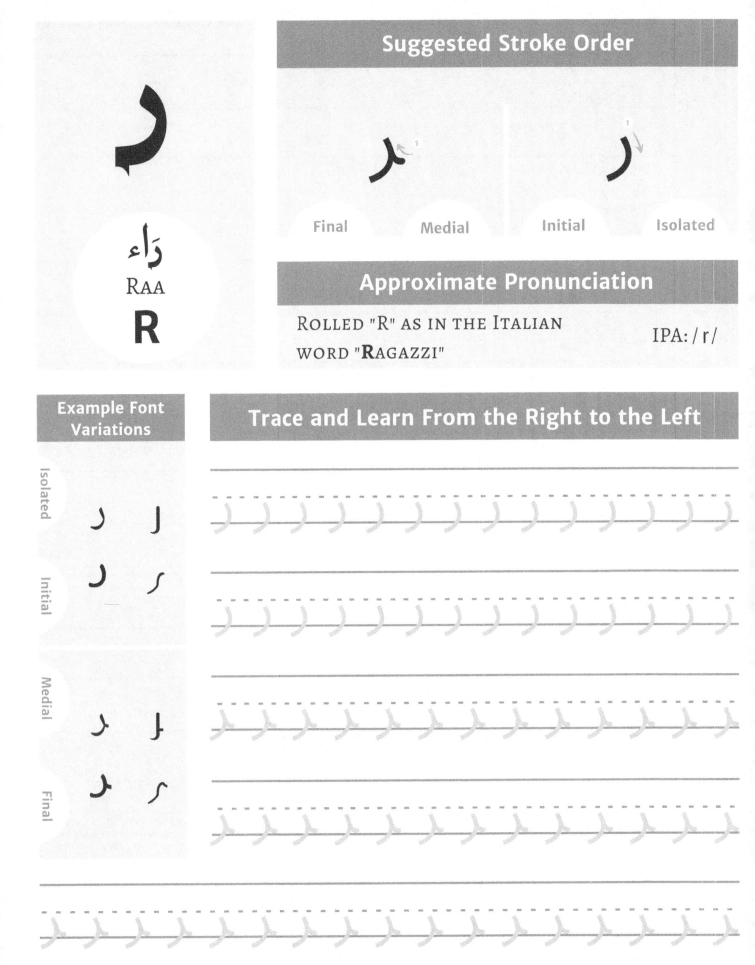

Final   Medial   Initial   Isolated

Approximate Pronunciation

ROLLED "R" AS IN THE ITALIAN WORD "**R**AGAZZI"

IPA: /r/

Trace and Learn From the Right to the Left

Isolated

Initial

Medial

Final

ز

 زَاي

ZAA

Z

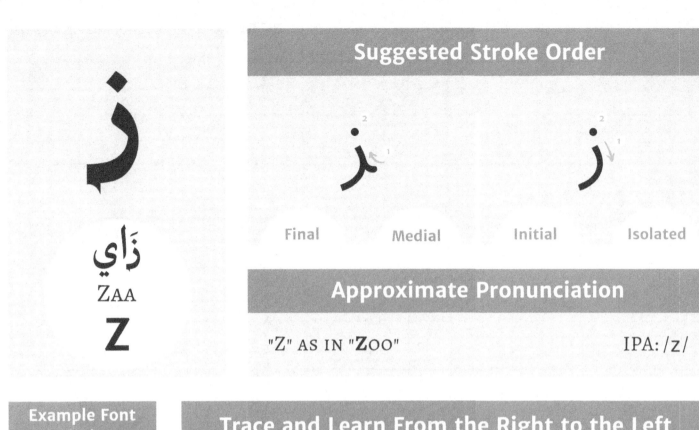

Final   Medial   Initial   Isolated

Approximate Pronunciation

"Z" AS IN "ZOO"   IPA: /z/

Example Font Variations

Trace and Learn From the Right to the Left

Isolated   ز ز

Initial   ز ﻧ

Medial   ﻟ ﻧ

Final   ﻟ ﻧ

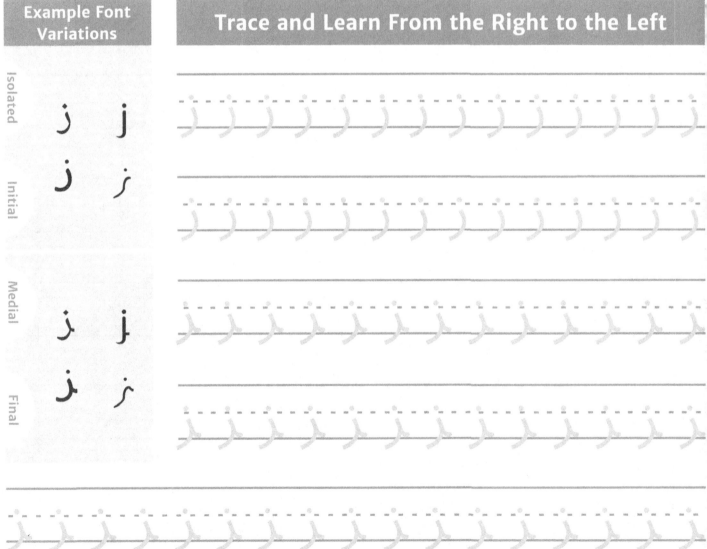

زِ زِ زِ زِ زِ زِ زِ زِ زِ زِ زِ زِ زِ زِ زِ زِ زِ زِ زِ

زِ

زِ

زِ

زُ زُ زُ زُ زُ زُ زُ زُ زُ زُ زُ زُ زُ زُ زُ زُ زُ

زُ

زُ

زُ

زُ

SEEN

S

Final   Medial   Initial   Isolated

Approximate Pronunciation

"S" AS IN "SUN"   IPA: /s/

Example Font Variations	Trace and Learn From the Right to the Left
Isolated	
Initial	
Medial	
Final	

ﺱ ﺱ ﺱ ﺱ ﺱ ﺱ ﺱ ﺱ ﺱ

ﺱ

ﺱ

ﺱ

ﺳﺳ ﺳﺳ ﺳﺳ ﺳﺳ ﺳﺳ ﺳﺳ ﺳﺳ ﺳﺳ

ﺳﺳ

ﺳﺳ

ﺳﺳ

ﺳﺳ

ش

شِين
SHEEN
Sh

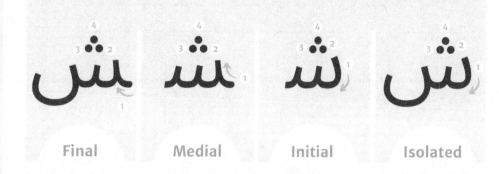

Final Medial Initial Isolated

Approximate Pronunciation

"SH" AS IN "**SH**IN" IPA: / ʃ /

Isolated	ش ش / ش ش
Initial	شـ شـ / شـ شـ
Medial	ـشـ ـشـ / ـشـ ـشـ
Final	ـش ـش / ـش ـش

Trace and Learn From the Right to the Left

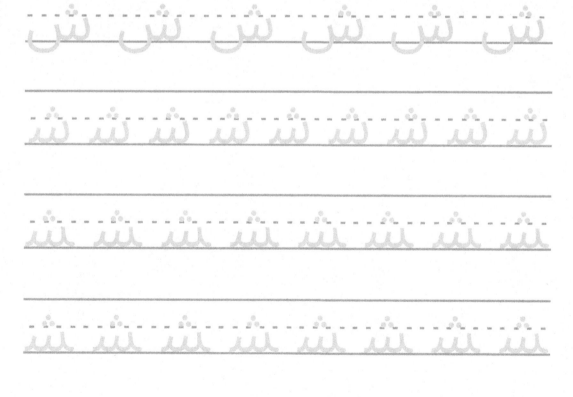

ش ش ش ش ش ش ش ش ش ش ش ش ش

ش

ش

ش

ثـ ثـ ثـ ثـ ثـ ثـ ثـ ثـ ثـ ثـ ثـ ثـ

ـثـ

ـثـ

ـثـ

شش شش شش شش شش شش شش شش شش شش

شش

شش

شش

ﺵ ﺵ ﺵ ﺵ ﺵ ﺵ ﺵ ﺵ

ﺵ

ﺵ

ﺵ

ﺵ

صَاد

ṢAAD

Ṣ

Final Medial Initial Isolated

Approximate Pronunciation

"S" AS IN "**S**AW" IF YOU PRONOUNCE IT
WHILE CONSTRICTING YOUR THROAT

IPA: /sˤ/

Example Font Variations

Trace and Learn From the Right to the Left

Isolated

Initial

Medial

Final

ض ض ض ض ض ض ض ض ض ض

ض

ض

ض

ض ض ض ض ض ض ض ض ض ض

ض

ض

ض

ض

ص ص ص ص ص ص ص ص ص ص ص ص ص

ص

ص

ص

ﺿ ﺿ ﺿ ﺿ ﺿ ﺿ ﺿ

ﺿ

ﺿ

ﺿ

ﺿ

ضاد
ḌAAD
Ḍ

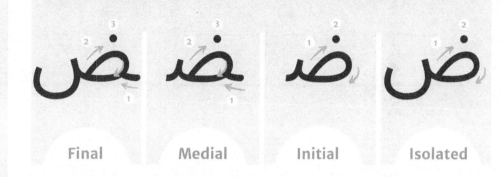

Final | Medial | Initial | Isolated

Approximate Pronunciation

"D" AS IN "DAWN" IF YOU PRONOUNCE
IT WHILE CONSTRICTING YOUR THROAT

IPA: /dˤ/

Example Font Variations

Isolated ض ض / ض ض

Initial ض ض / ض ض

Medial ض ض / ض ض

Final ض ض / ض ض

Trace and Learn From the Right to the Left

ض ض ض ض ض ض ض ض

ض

ض

ض

ض ض ض ض ض ض ض ض

ض

ض

ض

ض

ض ض ض ض ض ض ض ض ض ض ض ض

ض

ض

ظ

ض ض ض ض ض ض ض ض

ض

ض

ض

ض

ط

ظاء

ṬAA

Ṭ

Suggested Stroke Order

Final   Medial   Initial   Isolated

Approximate Pronunciation

"T" AS IN "STALL" IF YOU PRONOUNCE
IT WHILE CONSTRICTING YOUR THROAT

IPA: /tˤ/

Example Font Variations

Isolated

Initial

Medial

Final

Trace and Learn From the Right to the Left

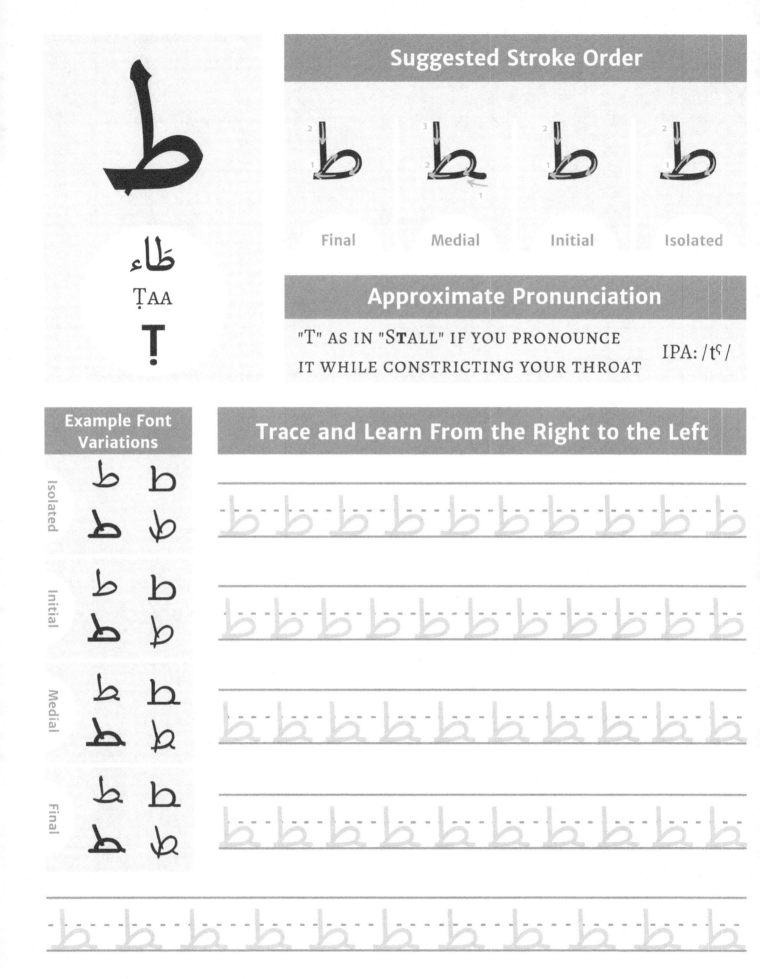

ь ь ь ь ь ь ь ь ь ь ь ь ь ь

ь

ь

ь

ь ь ь ь ь ь ь ь ь ь ь ь ь ь

ь

ь

ь

ь ь ь ь ь ь ь ь ь ь ь ь ь ь ь ь

ь

ь

ь

ь ь ь ь ь ь ь ь ь ь ь ь ь ь ь ь

ь

ь

ь

ь

ظَاء

ZAA

Ẓ

Suggested Stroke Order

Final · Medial · Initial · Isolated

Approximate Pronunciation

"TH" AS IN "FATHER" IF YOU PRONOUNCE IT WHILE CONSTRICTING YOUR THROAT

IPA: /ðˤ/

Example Font Variations

Isolated

Initial

Medial

Final

Trace and Learn From the Right to the Left

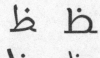

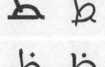

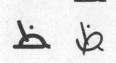

ظ ظ ظ ظ ظ ظ ظ ظ ظ ظ ظ

ظ

ظ

ظ

ظ ظ ظ ظ ظ ظ ظ ظ ظ ظ ظ

ظ

ظ

ظ

ظ

ظ ظ ظ ظ ظ ظ ظ ظ ظ ظ ظ ظ ظ

ظ

ظ

ظ

ظ ظ ظ ظ ظ ظ ظ ظ ظ ظ ظ ظ ظ

ظ

ظ

ظ

ظ

ع

عَيْن

'AYN

ء

| Final | Medial | Initial | Isolated |

Approximate Pronunciation

LIKE THE GUTTURAL "R" IN THE
GERMAN WORD "MUTTER"

IPA: /ʕ/

Example Font Variations

Trace and Learn From the Right to the Left

Isolated

ع ع
ع ع

Initial

ع ع
ڡ ع

Medial

ع ع
ع ع

Final

ع ع
ع ع

ع ع ع ع ع ع ع ع ع ع ع ع ع ع ع ع

ع

ع

ع

ح ح ح ح ح ح ح ح ح ح ح ح ح ح ح ح

ح

ح

ح

ح

ۇ ۇ ۇ ۇ ۇ ۇ ۇ ۇ ۇ ۇ ۇ ۇ ۇ ۇ ۇ

ۇ

ۇ

ۇ

ع ع ع ع ع ع ع ع ع ع ع ع ع ع ع

ع

ع

ع

ع

غَين

GHAYN

Gh

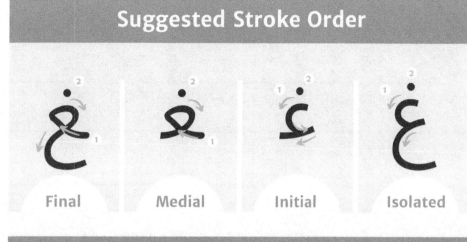

Final · Medial · Initial · Isolated

Approximate Pronunciation

SIMILAR TO THE G AS IN THE HINDI NAME "GANDHI"

IPA: /ɣ/

Example Font Variations

Isolated · Initial · Medial · Final

Trace and Learn From the Right to the Left

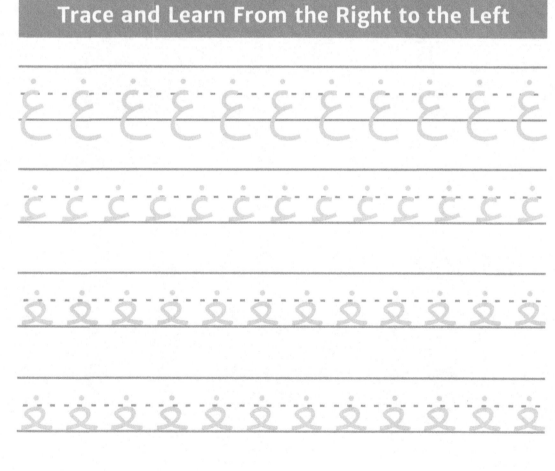

ع ع ع ع ع ع ع ع ع ع ع ع ع ع ع

غ

غ

غ

ح ح ح ح ح ح ح ح ح ح ح ح ح ح ح

خ

خ

خ

غـ غـ غـ غـ غـ غـ غـ غـ غـ غـ غـ غـ غـ غـ غـ

غـ

غـ

غـ

غ غ غ غ غ غ غ غ غ غ غ غ غ غ

غ

غ

غ

غ

فَاء

FAA

F

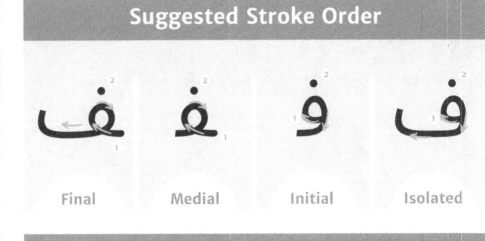

Final	Medial	Initial	Isolated

Approximate Pronunciation

"F" AS IN "FALL" IPA: / f /

Trace and Learn From the Right to the Left

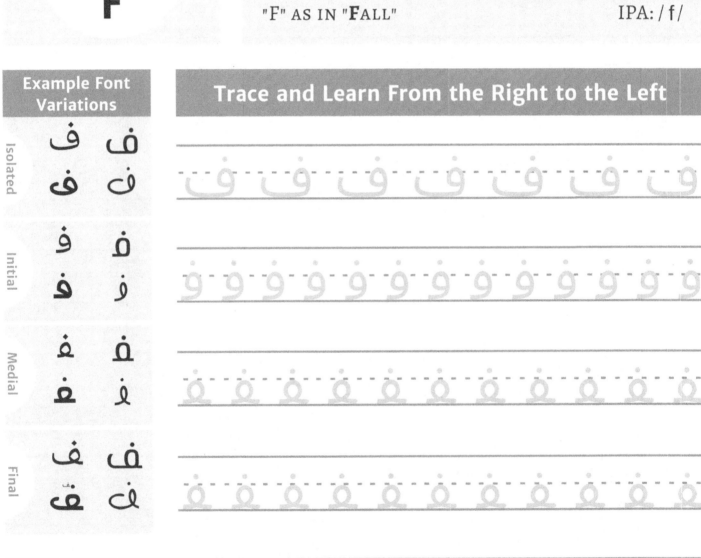

Isolated

Initial

Medial

Final

ف ف ف ف ف ف ف ف ف

ف

ف

ف

ؤ ؤ ؤ ؤ ؤ ؤ ؤ ؤ ؤ

ؤ

ؤ

ؤ

ؤ

ؤ ؤ ؤ ؤ ؤ ؤ ؤ ؤ ؤ ؤ ؤ ؤ ؤ ؤ ؤ ؤ

ؤ

ؤ

ؤ

ـؤ ـؤ ـؤ ـؤ ـؤ ـؤ ـؤ ـؤ ـؤ

ـؤ

ـؤ

ـؤ

ـؤ

ق

قَاف

QAAF

Q

 Final   Medial   Initial   Isolated

Approximate Pronunciation

"C" AS IN "CALL", BUT PRONOUNCED CLOSER TO YOUR THROAT

IPA: /q/

Example Font Variations

Isolated	ق ق / ق ق
Initial	ﻗ ﻗ / ﻗ ﻗ
Medial	ﻘ ﻘ / ﻘ ﻘ
Final	ﻖ ﻖ / ﻖ ﻖ

Trace and Learn From the Right to the Left

ق ق ق ق ق ق ق ق ق

ﻗ ﻗ ﻗ ﻗ ﻗ ﻗ ﻗ ﻗ ﻗ

ﻘ ﻘ ﻘ ﻘ ﻘ ﻘ ﻘ ﻘ

ﻖ ﻖ ﻖ ﻖ ﻖ ﻖ ﻖ ﻖ

ق ق ق ق ق ق ق ق ق

ق ق ق ق ق ق ق ق ق ق ق ق

ق

ق

ق

ؤ ؤ ؤ ؤ ؤ ؤ ؤ ؤ ؤ ؤ ؤ ؤ

ؤ

ؤ

ؤ

ةٌ ةٌ ةٌ ةٌ ةٌ ةٌ ةٌ ةٌ ةٌ ةٌ ةٌ ةٌ ةٌ ةٌ ةٌ

ةٌ

ةٌ

ةٌ

قٌ قٌ قٌ قٌ قٌ قٌ قٌ قٌ قٌ قٌ قٌ

قٌ

قٌ

قٌ

قٌ

كَاف

KAAF

K

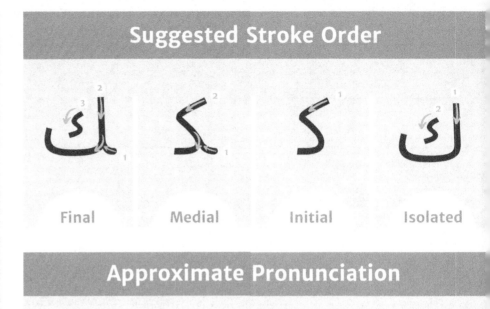

Final   Medial   Initial   Isolated

Approximate Pronunciation

"C" AS IN "CAT"   IPA: /k/

Example Font Variations

Trace and Learn From the Right to the Left

Isolated	
Initial	
Medial	
Final	

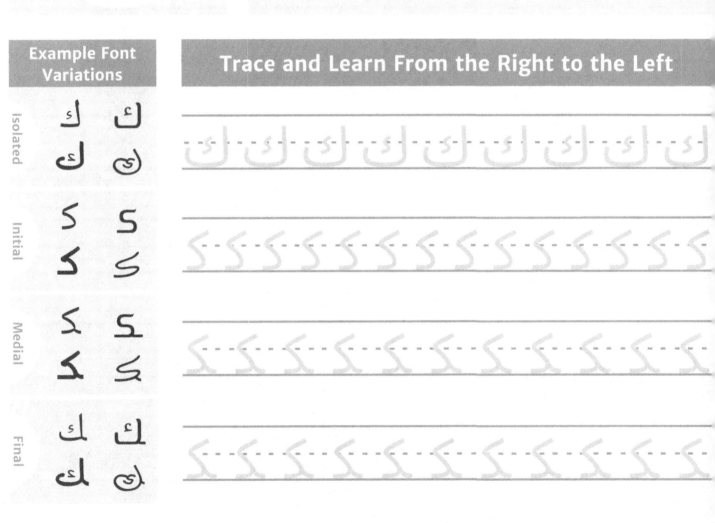

ك ك ك ك ك ك ك ك ك ك ك ك ك ك

ك

ك

ك

ک ک ک ک ک ک ک ک ک ک ک ک ک ک

ک

ک

ک

ک

ک ک ک ک ک ک ک ک ک ک ک ک ک ک

کـ

کـ

کـ

ـکـ ـکـ ـکـ ـکـ ـکـ ـکـ ـکـ ـکـ ـکـ ـکـ ـکـ

ـك

ـك

ـك

ـك

لَامٌ

LAAM

L

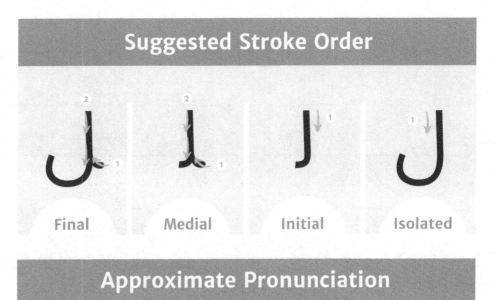

| Final | Medial | Initial | Isolated |

Approximate Pronunciation

"L" AS IN "LOVE"   IPA: / l /

Example Font Variations

	Isolated
	Initial
	Medial
	Final

Trace and Learn From the Right to the Left

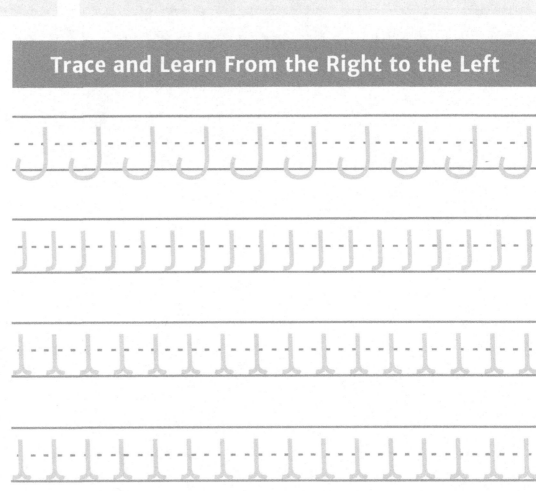

ميم

MEEM

M

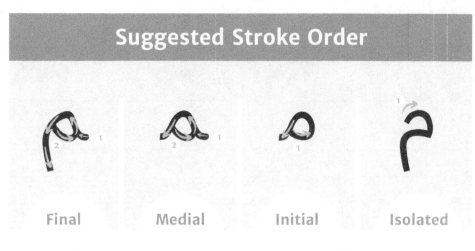

Final   Medial   Initial   Isolated

Approximate Pronunciation

"M" AS IN "MOTHER"   IPA: /m/

Example Font Variations	
Isolated	
Initial	
Medial	
Final	

Trace and Learn From the Right to the Left

a a a a a a a a a a a a a a

a

a

a

a a a a a a a a a a a a a a

a

a

a

a

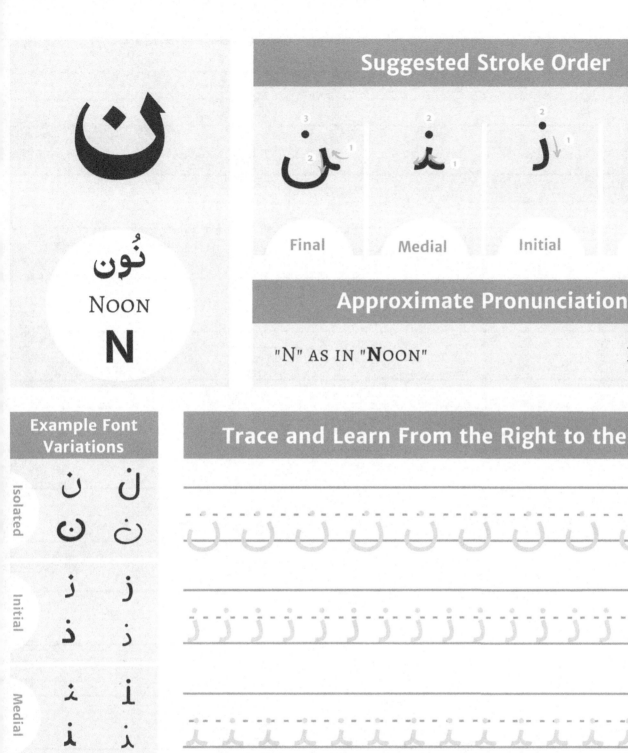

ن

نُون

NOON

N

Final · Medial · Initial · Isolated

Approximate Pronunciation

"N" AS IN "**N**OON"

IPA: /n/

Example Font Variations

Isolated

Initial

Medial

Final

Trace and Learn From the Right to the Left

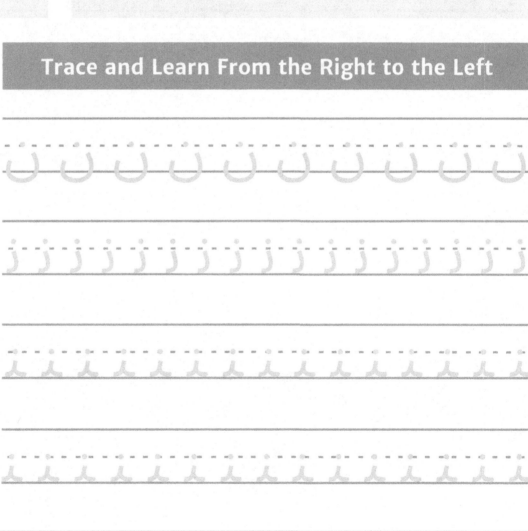

ن ن ن ن ن ن ن ن ن ن ن ن ن ن ن

ن

ن

ن

ز ز ز ز ز ز ز ز ز ز ز ز ز ز ز

ز

ز

ز

ز

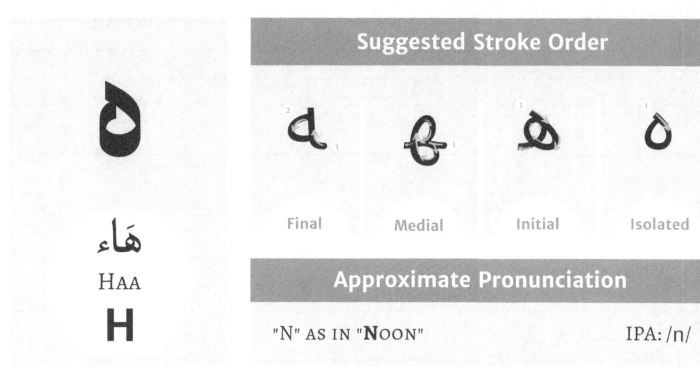

هَاء

HAA

H

Suggested Stroke Order

Final   Medial   Initial   Isolated

Approximate Pronunciation

"N" AS IN "**N**OON"   IPA: /n/

Example Font Variations

Trace and Learn From the Right to the Left

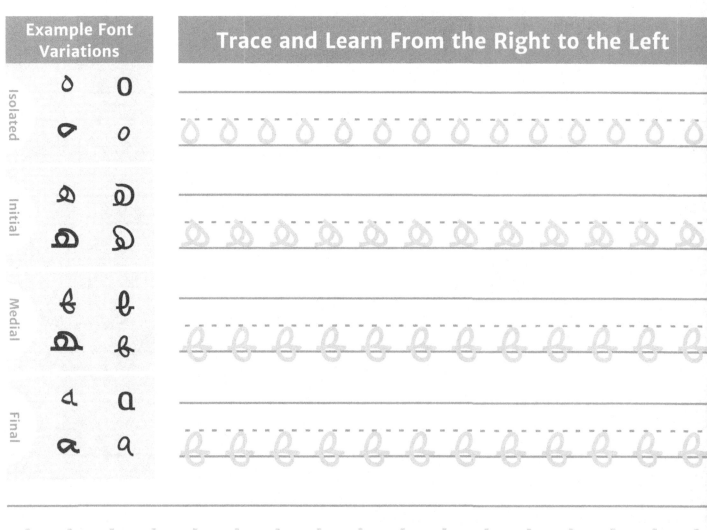

b b b b b b b b b b b b b b b

b

b

b

d d d d d d d d d d d d d d d

d

d

d

d

و

وَاو

WAAW

W

Approximate Pronunciation

"W" AS IN "**W**HAT"   IPA: /w/

"Oo" AS IN "Z**oo**"   IPA: /u:/

Example Font Variations

Isolated   و   و

Initial   و   و

Medial   و   و

Final   و   و

Trace and Learn From the Right to the Left

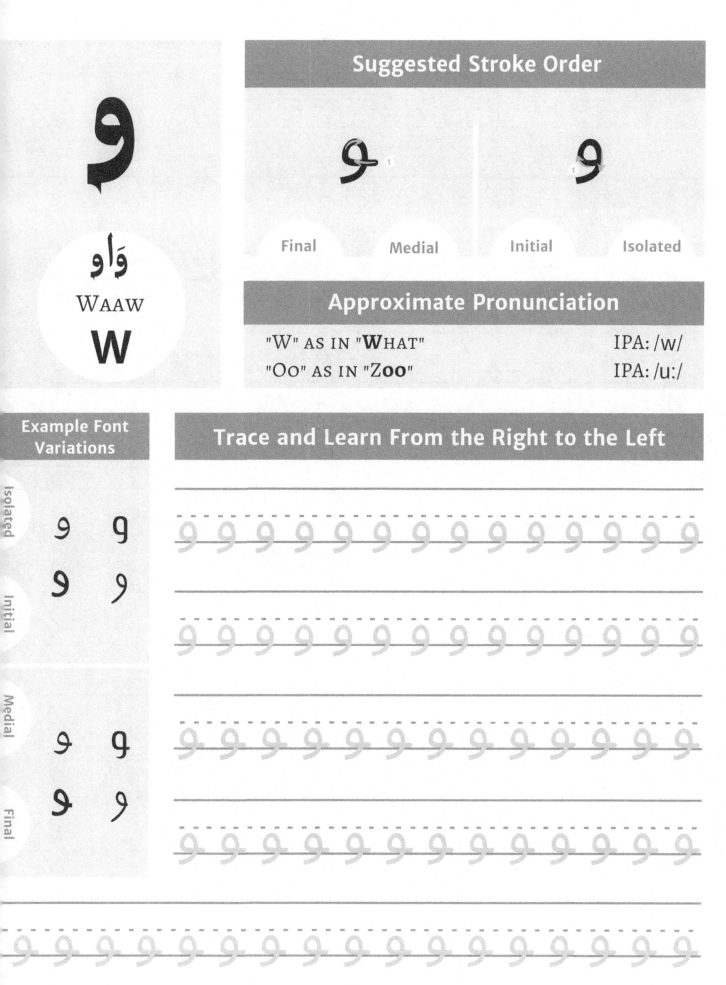

و و و و و و و و و و و و و و و و و و و

و

و

و

و و و و و و و و و و و و و و و و و و و

و

و

و

ي

يَاء

YAA

Y

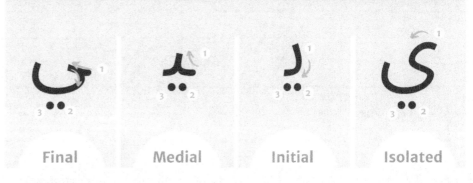

| Final | Medial | Initial | Isolated |

Approximate Pronunciation

"Y" AS IN "YOUNG"　　　　　　　　IPA: / j /

"EE" AS IN "SEE"　　　　　　　　　IPA: /i:/

Example Font Variations

	Isolated
	Initial
	Medial
	Final

Trace and Learn From the Right to the Left

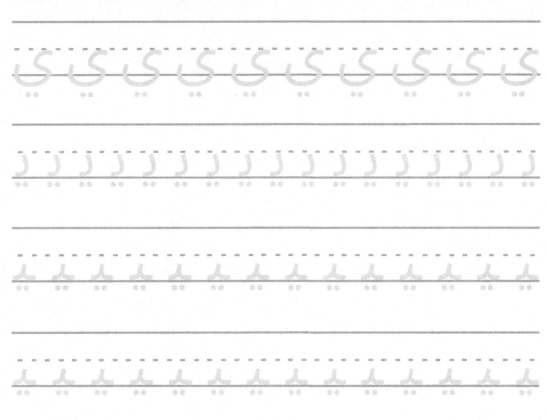

ى ى ى ى ى ى ى ى ى ى ى ى

ﯨ

ﯨ

ﯨ

ر ر ر ر ر ر ر ر ر ر ر ر ر ر ر ر ر ر

ﺮ

ﺮ

ﺮ

ﺮ

ء

صَاد
HAMZA
،

Hamza Carriers

'Alif Hamzah	Wāw Hamzah	Yā' Hamzah
Isolated / Initial	Isolated / Initial	Initial / Isolated
أ إ	ؤ	ئ ؤ
أ إ	ؤ	ئ ئ
Medial / Final	Medial / Final	Final / Medial

Approximate Pronunciation

GLOTTAL STOP LIKE IN THE WORD
"CO-OPERATE" OR IN "UH-OH"

IPA: /ʔ/

ء ء
ء ء

Trace and Learn the Hamza

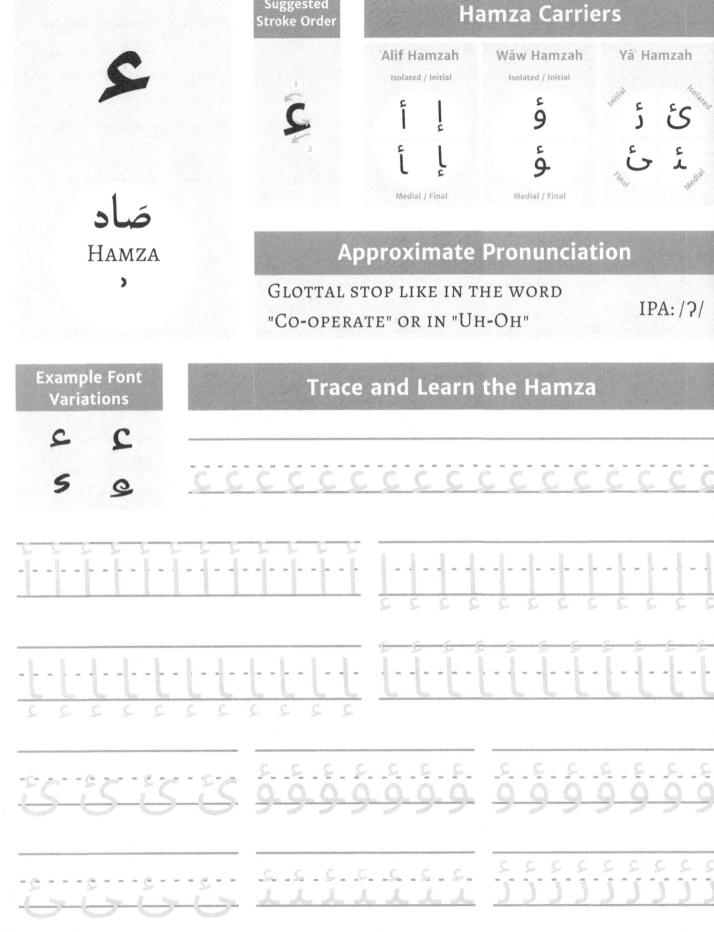

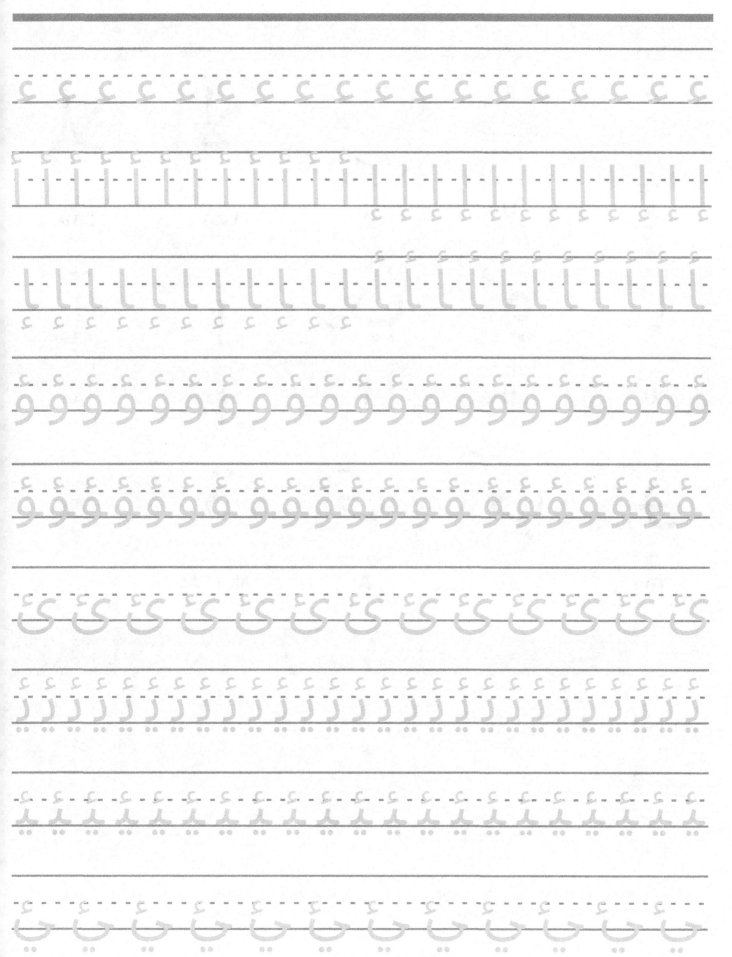

83

Vowels and Selected Special Characters

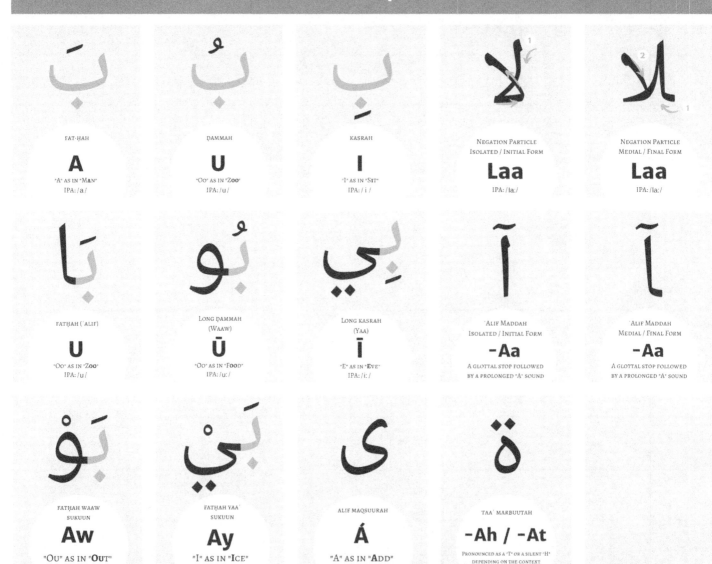

FAT-ḤAH	ḌAMMAH	KASRAH	Negation Particle ISOLATED / INITIAL FORM	Negation Particle MEDIAL / FINAL FORM
A	**U**	**I**	**Laa**	**Laa**
"A" AS IN "MAN"	"OO" AS IN "ZOO"	"I" AS IN "SIT"	IPA: /laː/	IPA: /laː/
IPA: /a/	IPA: /u/	IPA: /i/		
FATḤAH ('ALIF)	LONG ḌAMMAH (WAAW)	LONG KASRAH (YAA)	'ALIF MADDAH ISOLATED / INITIAL FORM	'ALIF MADDAH MEDIAL / FINAL FORM
U	**Ū**	**Ī**	**-Aa**	**-Aa**
"OO" AS IN "ZOO"	"OO" AS IN "FOOD"	"E" AS IN "EVE"	A GLOTTAL STOP FOLLOWED BY A PROLONGED "A" SOUND	A GLOTTAL STOP FOLLOWED BY A PROLONGED "A" SOUND
IPA: /u/	IPA: /uː/	IPA: /iː/		
FATḤAH WAAW SUKUUN	FATḤAH YAA' SUKUUN	ALIF MAQSUURAH	TAA' MARBUUTAH	
Aw	**Ay**	**Á**	**-Ah / -At**	
"OU" AS IN "OUT"	"I" AS IN "ICE"	"A" AS IN "ADD"	PRONOUNCED AS A "T" OR A SILENT "H" DEPENDING ON THE CONTEXT	

Additional Diacritical Marks

In the following pages you'll find ample space to train your ability to handwrite these vowels, special characters and diacritical marks. Feel free to photocopy these pages as needed.

لا لا لا لا لا لا لا لا لا لا لا لا لا لا لا لا

لا لا لا لا لا لا لا لا لا لا لا لا لا لا لا لا

لا لا لا لا لا لا لا لا لا لا لا لا لا لا لا لا

لا لا لا لا لا لا لا لا لا لا لا لا لا لا لا لا

لا لا لا لا لا لا لا لا لا لا لا لا لا لا لا لا

لا لا لا لا لا لا لا لا لا لا لا لا لا لا لا لا

نا نا نا نا نا نا نا نا نا نا نا نا نا نا نا نا

نا نا نا نا نا نا نا نا نا نا نا نا نا نا نا نا

نا نا نا نا نا نا نا نا نا نا نا نا نا نا نا نا

لا

لا

لا

لا

لا

لا

بَا

بَا

بَا

مُوْ

مُوْ

مُوْ

بِيْ

بِيْ

بِيْ

أَ

أَ

أَ

أَ

أَ

أَ

بَوْ

بَوْ

بَوْ

بَيْ

بَيْ

بَيْ

92

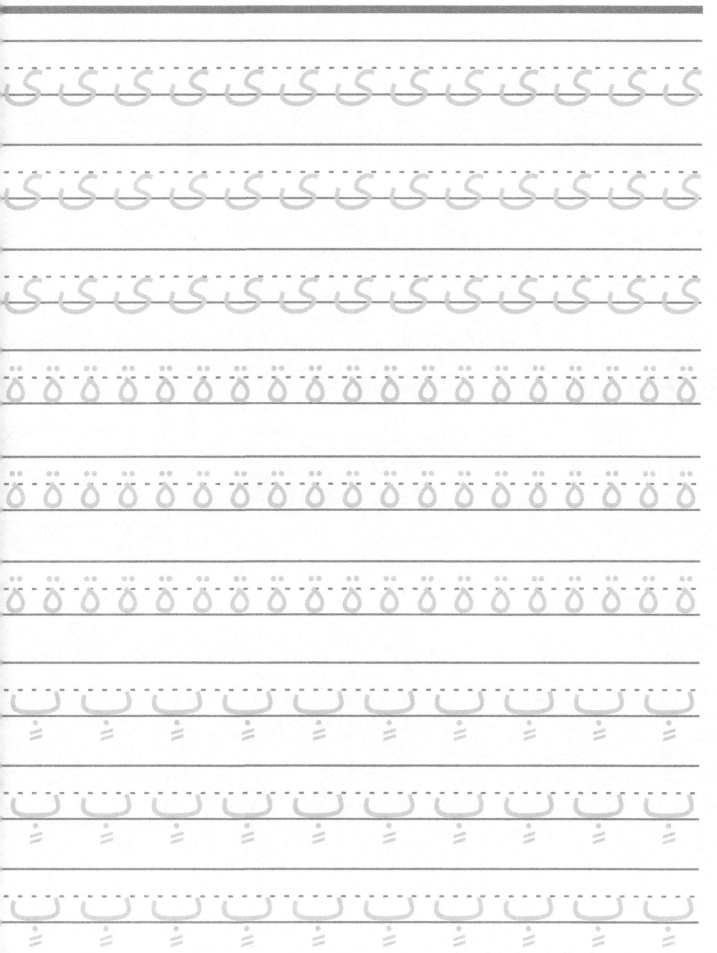

ى

ى

ى

ة

ة

ة

بْ ـبـ بـ

بْ ـبـ بـ

بْ ـبـ بـ

ثُبْ

ثُبْ

ثُبْ

ثِبْ

ثِبْ

ثِبْ

ثَبْ

ثَبْ

ثَبْ

Made in the USA
Las Vegas, NV
28 December 2023

83592948R00063